dedicated to:
....

....

....

celebrating *Life*

words of comfort

JIM McCANN, FOUNDER

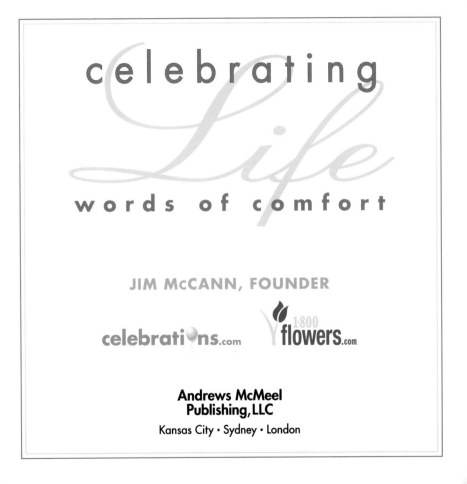

celebrati⦿ns.com 1·800 flowers.com

Andrews McMeel Publishing, LLC

Kansas City · Sydney · London

For information, write Andrews McMeel Publishing, LLC, an Andrews McMeel Universal company, 1130 Walnut Street, Kansas City, Missouri 64106

ISBN-13: 978-1-4494-0655-4

Library of Congress Control Number: 2010939800

11 12 13 14 15 SMA 10 9 8 7 6 5 4 3 2 1

www.andrewsmcmeel.com

ATTENTION: SCHOOLS AND BUSINESSES

Andrews McMeel books are available at quantity discounts with bulk purchase for educational, business, or sales promotional use. For information, please write to: Special Sales Department, Andrews McMeel Publishing, LLC, 1130 Walnut Street, Kansas City, Missouri 64106.

Project Manager and Editor: Heidi Tyline King

Designed by Alexis Siroc

Produced by SMALLWOOD & STEWART, NEW YORK CITY

Illustration credit information on page 70.

INTRODUCTION

WHEN I RAN A GROUP HOME for troubled teenagers in my early 20s, we took in a guy on an emergency basis. Kevin was a good-looking kid with a big personality, and almost instantly he became one of the favorites in the group. One night, as he was returning home, he was struck by a car and killed. More than ever before, I found myself in the role of a surrogate father, planning a wake and scrambling to notify any family or friends while at the same time, trying to stay strong for the rest of the boys in the home. That was perhaps the hardest of all. Most of these boys had experienced violence and suffered loss of unimaginable magnitude, and now, in what was supposed to be their last "safe place," tragedy had found them again. But somewhere between our anger and sadness, we managed to dress up and celebrate his life, pulling together through this shared experience in a way we never had before. In losing Kevin, we became a family.

Many years later, I was in Chicago on business when I received a phone call telling me that Carl, one of my oldest friends, had died suddenly of a heart attack. *Not Carl*, I thought. He was the tough guy, scrappy, always physically fit, a rock-solid New York policeman who had recently retired after 30 years on the job. His death shook me up. Carl left behind two sons, and a few years later when the youngest graduated from college, I had the honor of being commencement speaker. When he walked across the stage that day, I was filled with emotion. All this time I had thought Carl was gone but I realized in that moment that here, in front of me and very much alive, was his legacy, a son who would have made his father proud.

More recently, I had the deeply moving experience of being at my mother-in-law's side as she was dying. Mary was one special lady, the kind of person who made everyone feel welcomed and loved. Though we were all sad to see her go, our family was awed by how serene it was for her at the end, and we vowed to make her memorial service a celebration of her life. Afterward, a lady we had never met introduced herself to my wife, Mary Lou, and me and said she was a member of Mary's prayer group. "Mary told me," she said to us, "that she was ready to go anytime—that she had done the things she had wanted to do and that she was comfortable with whatever plan God had chosen for her."

Even now, to look back and remember the sense of peace this complete stranger gave to my wife and me during this time of loss leaves me speechless.

We all know firsthand how overwhelmed and underprepared we are as humans to deal with loss. Death breaks us open. It awakens an awareness of just how fleeting and fragile life really is. But even in the midst of heartbreaking grief, there always seems to be a light. It might be a faint flicker at first, especially when it takes all of our energy just to make it through those first hours, days, and weeks after losing someone we love. But with time, that light—that hope—grows stronger as we come to understand and celebrate the spirit of life.

ONE

SAYING GOOD-BYE

*The gods conceal from men
the happiness of death,
that they may endure life.* —LUCAN

∞

My mother always had high expectations, and I felt as though I never measured up. Needless to say, it affected our relationship. But then I had children of my own, and was overwhelmed by the rush of love I felt when they were born. I remember thinking, "This is how much my mother must love me. Who would have thought it!" Later, my mother was diagnosed with cancer, and as I held her like a newborn on that last day, I felt the same overwhelming rush of love and thought, "Oh my . . . this is how much I love her, too. Who would have thought it!" Looking back, I can see that from my first day to her last, love had been there always. —MARYBETH P.

*For death is no more than
a turning of us over from time to eternity.*

—WILLIAM PENN

May the road rise up to meet you,

May the wind be ever at your back.

May the sun shine warm upon your face

And the rain fall softly on your fields.

And until we meet again,

May God hold you in the hollow of his hand.

—IRISH BLESSING

*While we are mourning
the loss of our friend,
others are rejoicing to meet him
behind the veil.*

— JOHN TAYLOR (STATESMAN)

After our uncle's funeral, I was standing at the door mumbling the standard "Thanks for coming" to each guest. One elderly gentleman surprised me by answering with a grin, "Thanks for having me!" For a moment I just stood there, but then burst out laughing. Now at every funeral I attend, I tell the family, "Thanks for having me!" It brings a surprised reaction and laughter every time! —PAT S.

Only in the agony of parting
do we look into the depths of love.
—GEORGE ELIOT

∞

When I was six years old, I became sick at school. We didn't have a car at the time, so my mom picked me up and carried me the five long blocks home. I thought about that when I was visiting her in the nursing home, and I vowed to reciprocate by offering her the same safety and comfort that I had felt on that day long ago in her arms.

When she died, she was in my arms, and I like to think that I "ceremoniously" carried her home, staying close to her until she reached her final destination. —DIANE C.

Thy fate is the most common fate of all.
Into each life some rain must fall.

—HENRY WADSWORTH LONGFELLOW

Certain thoughts are prayers.
There are moments when, whatever
be the attitude of the body, the soul
is on its knees. —VICTOR HUGO

My dear friend Susie was mentally disabled and 10 years older than myself. She had been through some very rough times in her life, but she always had a smile on her face. She spent her final days mostly unresponsive, but on a rare occasion that she was semi-lucid, she looked at me and said, "I'm going to be an angel soon." Tears welled up in my eyes. Now, when I think about her, I can't help but think that she is watching over me, an angel in heaven, just as she was already here on earth. —JODI A.

Birth and death are not two different states but they are different aspects of the same state.

—MAHATMA GANDHI

There once was a woman who lost her child to disease. Crazy with grief, she stumbled through the city begging for medicine to bring her child back. When she came upon the Buddha, he told her he would give her the medicine she needed. He asked her to find a poppy from a house where no one had lost a loved one. In her quest, she found there was not even one such home. She realized that death is a fact of life, and that she was not alone in her grief. In this way, the Buddha awakened her wisdom, restoring peace to her heart. —TARO GOLD

Life is not separate from death.
It only looks that way.

—BLACKFOOT PROVERB

∞

I miss you so, but I thank you for the strength
that inherently resides inside the beautiful memories
I have of you. —LYNN I.

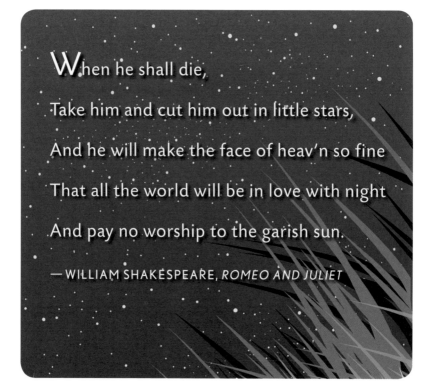

When he shall die,

Take him and cut him out in little stars,

And he will make the face of heav'n so fine

That all the world will be in love with night

And pay no worship to the garish sun.

—WILLIAM SHAKESPEARE, *ROMEO AND JULIET*

My grandfather was the strongest person I knew. But one night while I was in junior high, the two of us were alone in the living room, and the next thing I knew he was singing an old negro spiritual and crying. I started crying, too. When he finished, we looked at each other and smiled. Several weeks later, he died, and the first thing that came to mind was that moment. Even though I didn't know it at the time, it was that one sweet moment when we had said our good-byes. —ELEASE H.

∞

*I love you
from the ground up to God . . . forever.*

—WENDY T.

Death—the last sleep?
No, it is the final awakening.

—SIR WALTER SCOTT

Life is eternal and love is immortal
and death is only a horizon; and a horizon is
nothing save the limit of our sight.

—ROSSITER W. RAYMOND

TWO

HEALING

*What we have done for ourselves alone
dies with us; what we have done for others and
the world remains and is immortal.*

—ALBERT PIKE

After my mother passed, I realized that grief is often experienced alone. For me, focusing on even tiny moments of beauty pulled me out of what could otherwise have been a tailspin.   —DAGNY M.

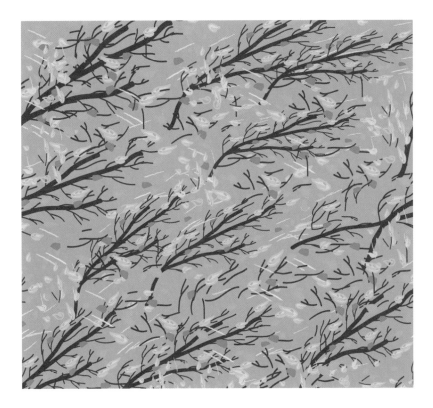

Even though my mother, Wanda, had been dead for three years, I was missing her more than ever on my birthday. She was always the first to call—at the crack of dawn—and she'd wake me by singing "Happy Birthday." As I went about my morning, I repeatedly asked for a sign to let me know that she was close. Later in the day, I had to make a quick phone call for an insurance quote and was put on hold. Moments later, when the agent returned to the line, she said enthusiastically, "By the way, happy birthday from Wanda!" She had noticed my date of birth—and her name was Wanda, too! Those words were the most beautiful gift I have ever received in my life. I love you, Mom, and take comfort in knowing that you are still here with us. —SUSAN C.

The mystery of love is greater than the mystery of death.

—OSCAR WILDE

Love is as strong as death.

—SONG OF SOLOMON 8:6

How vast a memory has love!

—ALEXANDER POPE

∞

My friend's mother died just before the birth of her baby. "The hardest part is knowing she won't be part of my baby's life," she said quietly. Feeling her pain, I gave her three balloons and a magic marker. "Here, write your mom a note. She's going to celebrate, too." She wrote the choices for the baby's name, the hospital, and the due date. We let the balloons go up in the air and watched until they were tiny specks. My friend now sends a balloon up at every family celebration so her mom is always part of her child's life. —MARIA D.

Write a letter to the person you miss. Even if you can't really mail it, the act of writing it down and sealing the letter will make you feel better. Take it from someone who has tried it. —JESS P.

My dad loved birds, in particular, cardinals. A few months after his passing, I was in my kitchen doing dishes. I looked up and saw a male cardinal sitting on a fence post, and I immediately thought of my dad. The cardinal is now a symbol to all five of his daughters. How we miss Dad, but knowing he is sitting on the sidelines, watching, makes us all smile. —PATTY A.

My father, who passed away eight years ago, was my hero, best friend, and sage. Even now, I hear his voice daily telling me to keep doing what is right, and to not be fearful of problems that arise. I believe him, because if I was able to survive losing a rock like him, there is nothing I can't do. —YESENIA C.

WHEN I WAS 15, *my mother passed away of cancer. We didn't have a funeral (her request) and my father gave my siblings and me one day off to cry and mourn. Then it was back to school and work. Needless to say, I was resentful of him. Last year, however, I lost two close friends and two beloved pets. I was devastated, but every day, I got up and went to work. I focused on the positive projects I was working on and the things I loved about my life. I won't say there weren't a lot of private tears, but having a focus and working late nights helped me come back into myself. Through it all, I have gained a new appreciation for how my father dealt with our loss. If I had taken weeks off, I think I could have easily drowned in self-pity. Some may say it's a way of avoiding grieving, but I would say it's a way to keep from getting lost in grief.* —DAGNY M.

The sorrow for the dead is the only sorrow
from which we refuse to be divorced. Every other
wound we seek to heal—every other affliction
to forget: but this wound we consider it
a duty to keep open—this affliction we cherish
and brood over in solitude.

—WASHINGTON IRVING

TRUST LIFE, AND IT WILL TEACH YOU,

IN JOY AND SORROW,

ALL YOU NEED TO KNOW.

—JAMES BALDWIN

 t is the will of God and Nature that these mortal bodies be laid aside, when the soul is to enter into real life; 'tis rather an embryo state, a preparation for living; a man is not completely born until he be dead: Why then should we grieve that a new child is born among the immortals? —BENJAMIN FRANKLIN

I lived out of state when my dad died and had a lot of guilt for not being there more when he was ill. When I returned home after attending his funeral, I started seeing my dad's head everywhere I went. You must understand—my dad always got the cheapest haircut in town. To him a $3 cut was a quality cut. Now, every man in town, it seemed, had the same white hair and bad haircut.

This went on for weeks until I finally realized it was an omen for me to stop feeling guilty. Once I came to that place, I stopped seeing the bad haircuts. From then on, it was only the heads of men who looked like him that I would see when I missed my dad. —ANON

I miscarried at 11 weeks, and while that was not very far into my pregnancy, this was a child we had been trying to conceive for 18 months. It was a devastating experience, and though my husband did his best to be supportive, in many ways I suffered alone. Through dealing with this loss and talking with so many women who have also miscarried, I have come to realize that part of healing is a two-part process: acknowledging the loss, but also honoring motherhood as a sacred path filled with crushing lows but also tremendous highs.

—LETA H.

Jack called.

I stared at the text. I was sitting in the doctor's office waiting for my mother's diagnosis. We knew something was wrong and had been for a long time. I had begged her to see the doctor, and she finally relented.

I looked at the text again. The only "Jack" I knew was my father, who had been dead for 14 years.

When the doctor finally called us in, he confirmed our suspicions, but said that at the end of a long road, there was hope. Walking out, I told my mom about the message. She smiled. "It was probably Dad," she said. "He's just letting me know everything is going to be okay." —PAT S.

Just as the two sides of a coin
are distinct yet inseparable,
our lives have a physical, tangible dimension
and a spiritual, intangible one.
We may differentiate
between body and mind,
but at their most fundamental level,
they are inseparable.

—TARO GOLD

Death is nothing at all—I have only slipped away into the next room.

Whatever we were to each other, that we are still.

Call me by my old familiar name, speak to me in the easy way which you always used.

Laugh as we always laughed together. Play, smile, think of me, pray for me.

Let my name be the household word that it always was.

Let it be spoken without effort. Life means all that it ever meant.

It is the same as it ever was; there is absolutely unbroken continuity.

Why should I be out of your mind because I am out of your sight?

I am but waiting for you, for an interval, somewhere very near just around the corner.

All is well. Nothing is past; nothing is lost.

One brief moment and all will be as it was before—

only better, infinitely happier and forever—

we will all be one together with Christ.

—CARMELITE MONASTERY PRAYER

THREE

REMEMBERING

On a clear day you can see forever.

—ANON

∞

MY MOTHER and I were reminiscing about my father and grandmother, both of whom had passed away. High school came up in the conversation and I pulled out my old yearbook. There, on a page in the back, my father had written, "To a lovely daughter, love you forever, Dad." And just above his message was one from my grandmother, written in Italian, "From your dear grandmother, infinite best wishes through your journey through life." I had read those words a thousand times, but I am positive that they were written for me to read now, after they were gone. They wanted me to always feel their presence. —VIVIAN L.

My mother, who is 85 years old, has a wonderful outlook on life: "Age doesn't make you old," *she says.* "Old is a state of mind." *This comes from a woman who got her PhD at the age of 80. Her brother, Harry, graduated college at 86. So while most people associate growing older in years with having one foot in the grave, I see it as an opportunity. Because of the example of the brave, admirable loved ones who have gone before me, I have no intention of quitting.* "Think young! Be young!" *is my motto, and old age simply gives me more time to live!*

—HOWARD S.

Absence diminishes little passions and increases great ones, just as the wind extinguishes candles and fans a fire.

—FRANÇOIS DUC DE LA ROCHEFOUCAULD

When I am overwhelmed by grief from losing my little girl, I follow her example by doing what she did to get by during those last weeks of her life: I breathe in the light and blow out the darkness. —WENDY T.

I lost my father unexpectedly when I was six years old. It has been almost 30 years now, and I sometimes get upset because the more time goes by, the more I seem to forget about him. Take the sound of his voice—I just can't remember what he sounded like or what he said. But I do remember his hands. When he would hold my tiny little six-year-old hand, it was almost as if his hands were swallowing mine. Now, whenever I feel alone, I close my eyes and think of his big, warm hands holding mine, and I feel safe once again. —LISA P.

There is a sacredness in tears.

They are not the mark of weakness,

but of power.

They speak more eloquently

than 10,000 tongues.

They are the messengers

of overwhelming grief,

of deep contrition,

and of unspeakable love.

— WASHINGTON IRVING

All the darkness in the world cannot extinguish the light of a single candle.

—SAINT FRANCIS OF ASSISI

My favorite uncle (more dear to me than my own father)
may be gone, but he lives on in my dreams.
I simply focus on dreaming about him right before
I go to sleep, and almost always, he shows up.
We'll talk and walk together just like we did before he died.
It helps so much that I can still feel him, especially when
I need and miss him most.

—MELISSA A.

Following my father's memorial, I noticed my mother bending over to pick up a penny. "Did you drop change, Mom?" She shook her head. "No, your dad is sending me love." I exchanged glances with my husband but my mother caught the look. "I'm not crazy. Ever since your father passed, I keep finding pennies. I found one at the cemetery. I found one when I cleaned out his clothes. I even found one in the garage when the neighbor came to buy his car. I like to think of them as your dad's way of letting me know he's thinking of me." From then on, our entire family began to find pennies everywhere, especially on milestone occasions or whenever we were missing Dad the most. We're certain it's just Dad sending us his love from above. —ANON

FUNNY HEADSTONE SAYINGS

"I told you I was sick!"

Here lies an atheist:
all dressed up and no place to go.

I was somebody.
Who, is no business of yours.

Blessed are the cracked
for they shall let in the light.

I would rather be here than in Texas.

She drank good ale, good punch and wine, and
lived to the age of 99.

When my son turned four, he began to ask questions about his grandpa up in heaven. I explained that he was way high in the sky, and that when it's sunny outside, it means that he is smiling down on us.

Well, my son took this literally and began talking to Grandpa throughout the day. He'd say things like, "It's too bright and the sun is hurting my eyes," or "Can you play with my friend's cat who is going to heaven, too?" I love that my son has a connection and place in his world for Grandpa. He thinks about him and feels free to talk to him at any time. And that's exactly what Grandpa would have wanted.

—FRANCES P.

WHEN MY FATHER DIED, many of his
business contacts living out of the country wanted to send their
condolences, but instead of flowers, they chose to send fruit
baskets—all of which came to the funeral home. After the service,
my mother, looking around in disbelief, said, "Do something
about this fruit! There is no way I can eat this much in a year!"

I looked at the baskets, then back at my mother. "What do
you mean do something?" I said.

She glared at me. "I am not dragging these baskets back to
Brooklyn! Hand it out as people leave."

So as people paid their respects and turned to go, my
brothers and I said, "Thank you for coming. Please take a
delicious piece of fruit for the ride home."

To this day, whenever I see a fruit basket, I get the giggles—
and a great memory of my father! —MARIA D.

TO LIVE IN HEARTS
WE LEAVE BEHIND
IS NOT TO DIE.

—THOMAS CAMPBELL

"Everything in this world has a solution, but death."
Sage words from my father,
and all the more ironic now that he is gone.

—YESENIA C.

My father, John Cooper, died a long, slow death. For eight years his wonderful light gradually dimmed until it passed from this world. I watched in wonder as my mother cared for him those long, painful years, particularly in the end, when she held his hand at his bedside and sang to him. My father's deepest concern as he lay dying was for my mother: He grieved knowing that he had to leave her. She loves him still, and I believe that he loves her from his grave. It was witnessing the devotion of my parents to each other that convinced me that love—unfathomable, miraculous, and mysterious love—does indeed last forever. —MARIA D.

As a teacher, I know the loss of a cherished grandparent is hard for a child to grasp, but my heart broke to watch my six-year-old nephew struggle in the weeks after he lost his grandpa. "I understand he can't come back, but I just wish I could hold his hand again," Jake said. Hoping to ease his grief, I hatched a plan. I took Jake to the bookstore to choose a special book in his grandfather's honor. Inside, we inscribed his grandfather's name and wrote, "Donated by his best pal and fishing buddy, his grandson Jake." Then together, we delivered it to his school library. Now, whenever Jake misses his grandpa, he knows there is a place he can go and touch a book that connects them. And the school was so moved by the idea that they created a special memorial book section in the library. —ANON

WHAT IS LIFE? It is the flash of a firefly in the night. It is the breath of a buffalo in the wintertime. It is the little shadow which runs across the grass and loses itself in the sunset. —CROWFOOT, BLACKFOOT WARRIOR

*Sometimes a man tells a story
so many times he becomes the story.
And that is what makes him immortal.*

—ANON

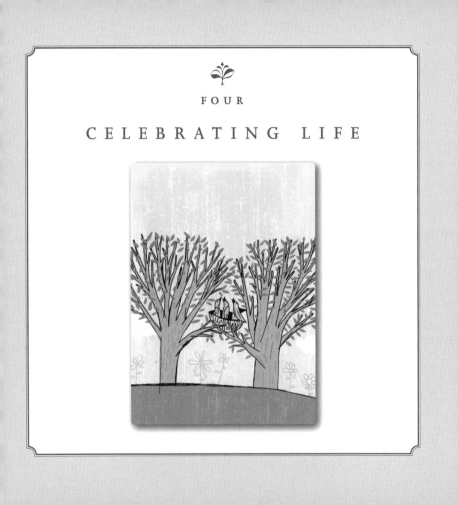

FOUR

CELEBRATING LIFE

My grandmother was the greatest. She was always happy. She never judged. She gave without asking for anything in return. She listened. Most of all, she loved me for me. My only hope in life is that when it's my time to go, I will have left others with the same feelings that my grandmother has left me: a lifetime of love and happy memories to carry them through until we are together once again. —MICHELLE M.

CELEBRATING LIFE

Death is the most beautiful adventure in life.

—CHARLES FROHMAN

∞

A human life is a story told by God.

—HANS CHRISTIAN ANDERSEN

MaryEllen, my sister and the oldest of eight siblings, was the glue that held our family together. After she died of ovarian cancer, we decided to celebrate her life by cooking her signature dishes and having a family dinner in her honor. For those of you who have lost someone dear, remember to celebrate the life once lived and to tell those who are still with you that you love them each day. —ANTHONY K.

*If a thing loves,
it is infinite.*

—WILLIAM BLAKE

Dad, the greatest gift you taught me was the gift of perseverance, optimism, and personal excellence. I thank you for the blessings of these gifts. They serve me well and are a beacon of light and beautiful way of remembering you always! —LYNN I.

It was six years ago that the doctors told me that my dearest Olivia Grace wouldn't make it . . . her brain tumor was back and inoperable. Forty-two days later, she took her last breath. I've always been afraid that her death would be bigger than her eleven years of life, so I try my best to honor her memory through the daily little things. Whenever I see a donation bucket, I contribute—just as she insisted when she was alive. —WENDY T.

Whenever my mother-in-law would hear of someone refusing to participate or do something on account of a loved one dying, she'd put her hands on her hips and say, "That's rubbish. Anybody knows: Life is for the living." —HEIDI K.

∞

People who make the most of life have no fear of death.

—TARO GOLD

One of the best gifts my husband, Jerry, ever gave me was flowers with a card that read, "You deserve to take pride in all you have done—I do!" After he died of a brain tumor, I kept it close to reread throughout some of my toughest days. It reminded me that I had a choice: I could pull the covers up over my head and pretend I didn't exist, or I could make a difference. Guess which one I chose? Soon after his death, I started a foundation and raised $100,000 for brain tumor research—all in honor of a special man who believed in me. —JOSEPHINE G.

❧ ❧ ❧ ❧ ❧ ❧ ❧ ❧ ❧ ❧ ❧

I saw the best headstone in Ireland:

DEATH LEAVES A HEARTACHE

NO ONE CAN HEAL,

LOVE LEAVES A MEMORY

NO ONE CAN STEAL.

—MICHAH R.

❧ ❧ ❧ ❧ ❧ ❧ ❧ ❧ ❧ ❧ ❧

Just after Dad passed away, Mom found a weathered treasure chest at one of his favorite liquidation stores. It was $10, which Dad, a bargain hunter, would have loved, but it had a timeless look to it. At home, Mom put the chest in front of the fireplace and over time, began adding special photos of him, letters he had written, his ID badge from work—even a favorite baseball cap that he wore fishing. Soon, this chest became our special place to remember Dad. Every year my sister writes him a letter and puts it inside. Our son draws pictures of family vacations and leaves them for Grandpa. It has become a place where we can go to remember the past and celebrate the future, knowing that Dad had a part in both. —HENRIETTA L.

When we lose someone,

it's easy to become focused on what we've lost. But that one loss is only a chapter of our lives. Each relationship is filled with so many complicated and fulfilling shared life experiences that we'd be remiss not to see that, together, there's an entire book to read. —NANCY H.

Who of you by worrying can add
a single hour to his life? Therefore do not
worry about tomorrow, for tomorrow
will worry about itself. Each day has enough
trouble of its own.

—MATTHEW 6:29

True love doesn't have a happy ending;
true love doesn't have an ending.

—ANON

One should count each day as a separate life.

—SENECA

My friend's dad, George, was the biggest New York Met fan there ever was. Not only did he have season tickets and know every stat, he bragged that he had never missed a game. When his son was born— you guessed it—George left the hospital in time to make it to Shea Stadium by the first pitch.

When George passed, his family received his cremated remains and debated what to do with the urn. The spring baseball season was about to begin and Bob's mom solved the problem by putting a shelf above the TV. She placed George's urn with a worn Met cap on top. George got the last laugh on death, for sure, because to this day he has still never missed a game! —PAT S.

I looked like an idiot. It was the middle of the night and I was kidnapping a rose bush that had been a gift from Dad to Mom on their 25th anniversary. For over 15 years the rose bush bloomed in my parents' garden. A year later, when Mom sold the house, she completely forgot about the bush and left it behind. When she finally remembered, I was the lucky one chosen to retrieve the bush.

After dragging it from my car to Mom's backyard, it looked pretty ragged. Still, she insisted that we replant it. Over the next year, I would find Mom looking out the window, staring at the bush. "It's not going to make it," I would tell her, but she refused to listen.

Then one October evening, just before the cool weather set in, I stopped by and found her in the backyard bending over the rose bush. "Look, new buds," she said joyfully. Sure enough, two small rose buds, defying all odds, were just starting to bloom. Mom smiled. "See, you never give up on love." —ANON

My mother was one of the women who never left the house without her makeup and her pearl earrings on. For over 43 years, Dad would tease her: "You are going to meet a secret admirer the moment my back is turned!" When Dad died suddenly of a heart attack, we all worried about Mom being alone. But she surprised us by getting a job. Every day she would take the bus to work and sit behind the driver. It wasn't long before she and the bus driver, Gus, were fast friends. A couple of years passed, and Mom went to Florida for a few weeks to help with the newest grandchild. When she returned and boarded the bus for the first time, Gus shook his head when she went to pay the fare. "Sorry Mrs. C, it's been paid." Confused, my mother asked, "By whom?" Gus smiled shyly. "I guess your secret admirer." Tears came to my mother's eyes as she took her seat in her usual place. From there, she could see his calendar and the red heart scribbled with the words "Mrs. C's back!" Mom smiled. She had met that secret admirer after all. —ANON

Winter always turns to spring.

—NICHIREN

When you were born, you cried
and the world rejoiced.
Live your life so that when you die,
the world cries and you rejoice.

—CHEROKEE SAYING

Enjoy yourself.
It's later than you think.

—CHINESE PROVERB

ILLUSTRATION CREDITS